ACKNOWLEDGMENTS

Dedicated to my amazing children, Evan and Linnea.

Thank you for bringing passion, joy, courage, love, truth, peace and belief into my life everyday.

I am so blessed. I love
you.

Mom xo

Cover Art By Les Luxemburger

DETOXING YOUR THOUGHTS

"Colour is food for the soul. It nourishes and heals us." *Angela Dacey*

As we live from day to day, our life is filled with many colourful pictures. These pictures form a gallery of our journey during this human existence. Some of the pictures may have different textures and designs. Some are beautiful in colour and filled with light and love. Others may be dark and dismal, revealing our deepest struggles. We create many pictures throughout the years. We are all eclectic, special and unique. No one has our thoughts, feelings or behaviours apart from us. Our story is *ours* alone and how we paint our life picture is up to us.

Ever since I can remember, colour grabbed my attention and mesmerized me. Remember when Crayola brought out its first big box of crayons? There were 64 colours with a crayon sharpener on the side of the box. The lid opened up as if you were opening a present filled with a colourful surprise. I still remember holding my breath as I opened the lid for the first time. This wasn't a package of 6 or even 12 crayons. This was the big kahoona of crayons. As I opened the lid, every colour I could possibly imagine was there, beckoning me to pick them out of the box. It was like there were families of colours. Blues of every colour: light blue, sky blue, royal blue, teal blue and turquoise. Greens resembling the colour of forests, green grass, limes, and even moss. There were colours I'd never seen before in a crayon such as the flesh colour to resemble our pale, Canadian skin, and there was even white.

Every colour seemed to have a story, a feeling, a purpose. My toughest decision was choosing which colour to take out of the box first. My eyes immediately landed on one colour, which stood out from the rest. I chose turquoise. It was like the ocean calling my name to come in for a swim. Out of 64 colours I chose turquoise....why?

As a young child I had no idea why turquoise was my first choice. My friends would all choose different colours as their first favourite. Now, as an adult, I fully understand. The colour therapy of turquoise, with that blue/green combination, has a purpose which has represented my life story; finding my voice, uncovering my true authenticity, speaking the truth and communicating from the heart.

Every obstacle in my life, every lesson I've learned, every struggle I've had to endure has led me back to the turquoise purpose.

What was the first colour you took out of the box? If you're unsure, close your eyes and picture a box full of colourful crayons. Which colour jumps out at you?

We will create many pictures throughout the years and we will attract different colours along with our life experiences, however, we are always in control of "choosing" which colours to add to our pictures.

It may be a new concept to you to hear you can "choose" your colours. So many of us feel that we are victim to life's circumstances. Our belief is that we are handed our colours by other people, and that we didn't choose this life or the colours in our hands. For example, many of my clients have stated that they weren't in control of an illness or witnessing the death of a loved one, and I completely understand that belief. However, how we choose to deal with these experiences and uncover the beauty they are teaching us in life is *our* choice.

It takes work to Live Life Colourfully.

Going through life with only the happy, sunny pictures is unrealistic. It's life and we are human, after all! We all have those negative thoughts and feelings. Whether you were teased at school, your parents divorced, you were abused, you moved from city to city, you grew up with more responsibilities than most kids, you were laughed at for trying, scolded for failing, blamed for things you didn't do, judged for being you – all these experiences, big or little, have created the framework for who you are today. These experiences are a part of life. They make us emotionally stronger, shape our personality, give us compassion for others, and make us strive to be a better person. However, many of us choose to live in the suffering that is hidden beneath the surface. Then one day we realize that those negative thoughts and feelings are hurting us. That old saying of, "What doesn't kill you will make you stronger" is true to a small degree. We learn from every experience and can choose to become a better person because of it. However, it fails to say, "Hanging on to the negative thoughts and feelings associated with that challenge, *will* kill you."

Our thoughts of not being good enough, smart enough, pretty enough, strong enough or worthy enough all stem from our stories and pictures. You weren't born with thoughts of being "less than." At one point in your life you decided that those words and expressions that were told to you, or the actions that were displayed towards you, were truth and so you believed them. No one told you to only believe the positive and not the negative. Your higher power, call it God, helped your spirit manifest into a tiny, perfect little body filled with nothing but love. You knew nothing else. As life began and you became more comfortable in your physical body, you started to feel and think in your own way while constantly absorbing thoughts and feelings that surrounded you from family, friends, school and your environment. You believed it when people said, "You were great," "Nice job," "You're so smart," "What a pretty little girl" or "What a sweet little boy." You also believed it when they said, "That's not good enough," "Why can't you be more like your sister?" "You didn't try hard enough," "No one will marry you" or "You'll never make it into university". These are just a few examples of the positive and negative statements you may have heard growing up. Can you remember what was said to you and which statements you absorbed? We became so comfortable believing those words that we still fail to realize that we have the right – and the power – to discard other people's words.

While each positive comment absorbed into our system, so did the negative comments. This creates a problem as thoughts and feelings hold energy. Maya Angelau says, "Words are things. They live in your furniture, your wallpaper, your clothing and in you." That's powerful. We all need to remember that words are things! The positive words create positive thoughts and feelings, however the negative words create negative thoughts and feelings. When positive thoughts and feelings are absorbed into our system it feeds our energy system. It's our energetic vitamins and minerals feeding our body with passion, joy, courage, balance, truth, inner peace, belief, love, and total body health. When the negative thoughts and feelings become absorbed into our system it's like eating an unhealthy diet for years. Our system will begin to shut down with the creation of fear, expectations, judgment, guilt, excuses, blame, denial, hatred, and disease. We choose what food to feed our body on a regular basis, but we rarely focus on what thoughts and feelings to feed and nourish our life. Our physical, mental, emotional and spiritual health is affected by this choice.

The good news is that the world is changing. Awareness is the key to healing and we're becoming a society that's far more aware that we need to bring peace to our inside world as well as our outside world. We now have the self-help industry booming as a multi billion dollar industry. We're looking for change, we're looking to heal and we're looking to prevent disease. And guess what? *You* can help in this awareness! *You* can help to bring peace, love and joy into the world. How? You can begin by taking care of yourself! You just need to become aware and take action to make a difference for yourself.

"I'll take care of me for you. You take care of you for me." Unknown.

It's time! Only sixty years ago, women were seen as mothers, caregivers and nurturers within their family unit. Nowadays we're still seen in this role, but we're also seen as entrepreneurs, CEOs, organizers, volunteers, planners, providers and protectors. More than 77 per cent of women are in the workforce compared to 39 per cent in 1950. June Cleaver from Leave It To Beaver barely exists anymore. On the one hand this is great! We've shown the world that we're capable, strong, intelligent and hard working while still being loving, caring and nurturing. However, now more than ever, we are focusing more on being a human "doing" instead of focusing on being a human "being" and this is creating much dis-ease in our bodies. We are exhausted physically, mentally, emotionally and spiritually. The Division of Cancer Prevention and Control states that in 2007 330,509 women died from heart disease, 223,044 women died from respiratory disease, and 40,954 women died from breast cancer. That's a total of 594,507 women! People, we need to stop this and we can if *you* start healing those negative thoughts and feelings! You are in control of your destiny.

Please note that this information is applicable for men too! We can all choose our thoughts, feelings and behaviours. Throughout my 25+ years working in this industry, I've personally found more women to be open to changing their inner world than men. However, I believe that since 2012, the energy has been shifting and more men are tuning into their personal power of health on all levels.

All it takes is openness and awareness. That's the first step. When you're open to healing and aware that you own a negative thought, only then can you take steps to heal that energy. Without awareness, you won't know what to heal. Let me explain how I became aware and healed part of my story.

"Don't wait for the storm to pass, learn to dance in the rain." Vivian Greene
I had a great family, great upbringing and lived what I'd call a

normal life. We had dogs, a pool, lots of friends, and went to school in the same neighbourhood from kindergarten to grade 12. I met my husband in high school and all in all it seemed like a normal, simple life. However, like everyone, I had a deeper story. Buried deep beneath my surface was a story of sexual abuse. I'd been abused by two different young men while I was between the ages of 7-10 and I forgot about those experiences until I started becoming sexually active with my boyfriend. The flashbacks began, reminding me of the experiences. Those negative thoughts and feelings created a complete lack of self-worth within me, including a depression and a feeling of not wanting to be here in this existence. After two years of dealing with the memories and the negativity, and being in a place of constant emotional heaviness, I remember saying to myself that I had a choice. I could either continue feeling all the pain or I could forgive these two young men for their actions, as they must have been pretty messed up themselves to commit an act like this. I chose forgiveness. I still remember the day that I admitted to my boyfriend that I had forgiven these two people. The room started turning a gorgeous shade of pink. Everything glowed and I felt that the ton of invasive, invisible hands on my body were now being lifted away one by one. Suddenly, I felt free! I could breathe again, my body felt peaceful, and I felt alive! The pink colour that was infused into my room was filled with love giving me a gigantic hug telling me, "*Yes*, forgiveness is the key." That was my turning point in life and it began at the age of 18. It was also the story that would create the framework for years and years of helping others detox their thoughts, find forgiveness, unconditional love, authenticity and compassion. Through a retail store I owned for seven years, to the counseling, training with my own line of courses, professional speaking and healing I've done for over 25 years, this story created my life journey and I feel so blessed to have experienced it. If I'd chosen to continue living with the pain, I would have continued to have terrible endometriosis, irritable bowel syndrome and migraine headaches. I'm now healed of those ailments as a result of detoxing my thoughts. To top it off, I increased my intuition and began using my spiritual gifts everyday. I did it, so you can too! The key is awareness and following through the actions of healing one step at a time. Your life isn't over. More pictures still need to be painted. It's up to you how you'd like to paint on the canvas. Experiences happen but you decide how to colour the creation.

In this book I'm going to guide you through the first key, which is awareness. We'll discuss thoughts and feelings, which ones are positive, and which are negative. I'll give you step-by-step guidance to begin seeing which negative energies you need to let go of to find total body health and happiness. All you have to do is commit to reading this book. Don't get to chapter 3 and then put it down. The time is *now*. Changes need to happen *now*. Are you happy in life? Are you healthy in life? Do you crave more passion, more love, more acceptance, more guidance and direction? Then congratulations! You purchased the right book. Remain open and enjoy the process.

WARNING: Your openness and awareness is going to lead to healing. So many people will be affected by your changes. Some will appreciate your effort and applaud your personal work. Those are the people you want to surround yourself with as they will support you in the ups and downs that may come with your inner healing. Others may feel threatened or scared of the "new" you or feel like you're changing and they are going to be judged if they don't change along with you. Please remember that they're reacting in a certain way due to "their" personal pictures. You need to focus on you and only you and God bless the others. Be the role model to those people. Even if it's your spouse or best friend, they have their own story and journey. They will become aware when they are ready for change.

AWARENESS

*Only by much searching and mining are gold and diamonds obtained,
and man can find every truth connected with his being if he will dig
deep into the mine of his soul."*
James Allen

In life, I believe we have 4 stages of wellness and illness, which directly affects our chakra system (or energy system). Chakra is a Sanskrit word meaning "Spinning Wheel of Energy." Details about the chakras will be discussed shortly but right now know that our chakras are connected to our physical, mental, emotional and spiritual state, and health.

Stage 1 – We spiritually / energetically have adopted thoughts and feelings

Stage 2 – We begin to feel those thoughts and feelings

Stage 3 – We mentally process our thoughts and feelings

Stage 4 – Our physical body reacts to the positive or negative influence.

Wellness = POSITIVE

Stage 1) Our thoughts and feelings hold positive energy, such as happiness, joy and love

Stage 2) We have a chakra energy system that is constantly spinning, combining our physical, mental, emotional and spiritual energies all working harmoniously together

Stage 3) Our physical body is in tip top shape and our organs are all functioning properly. We are healthy

Stage 4) We are able to live a long, healthy life

Illness = NEGATIVE

Stage 1) Our thoughts and feelings are holding onto negative energies, such as anger, fear, blame

Stage 2) Our chakra system experiences energy blocks from the negativity which causes some chakras to spin slowly while others spin quickly, leading to imbalances

Stage 3) Our spiritual, emotional and mental self has tried to tell us there is a problem but we weren't listening so our physical body starts to show us in ways such as digestive issues, sore throats, heart palpitations, headaches, sore joints and more.

Stage 4) Our physical body will deteriorate and terminate if healing does not take place.

Both the Wellness and Illness stages have the same 4 components. One component is focusing on positivity and the other on negativity. Each one focuses on thoughts, feelings, chakras, and ultimately, how healthy our physical self is doing considering the circumstances.

I've been mentioning that Awareness is the first step to success with detoxing your thoughts. We have to be aware of how our thoughts and feelings are functioning so that we can pinpoint the problem and begin to make changes in order to make a difference. If you're unsure of your thoughts and feelings, watch your actions. Actions will describe what is being processed in the mind and the heart. I'll share an example.

I had a client who loved being a stay-at-home mom. I'll call her Cindy. Cindy was an excellent playmate for her two children as she'd get down on the floor and play for hours as if she was still a child. When she was in this space, she was laughing, joyful and always smiling. Stress didn't seem to exist when Cindy focused on having a good time with her kids and using her creative imagination. However, when Cindy had to take care of household chores, such as doing the laundry, cooking supper and making the beds, her personality changed. Her actions became harsh. She'd smash the dishes into the cupboard, yell at the bed sheets when they wouldn't fit on the corners of the bed, make loud sighs, and snap at her children when they asked her a question. Cindy's actions became more negative. She seemed angry and upset instead of stress free and happy. During the angry times, Cindy became exhausted compared to the abundance of energy she seemed to have when in play mode with her kids. Cindy's actions demonstrated that somehow her thoughts and feelings were no longer positive but negative. Now she needed to understand why so that her physical body wouldn't break down as a result.

Awareness is usually the last step that people take. Their actions speak louder than words and to look inside and discover why their actions are negative takes work and most people avoid that. Unfortunately, time goes on and people usually need their physical body to begin screaming for help before they realize that there is a problem and commit to making a change.

It wasn't until Cindy's daughter said, "Mommy, why are you always mad at the dishes?" that she saw a side of her that she didn't know was there. After that comment, Cindy noticed her other daughter making her bed and yelling at the sheets, complaining that they weren't going on right. Cindy could now see how different she became when she was taking care of responsibilities compared to just being in the moment, playing with her children. Luckily, Cindy was open enough to become aware of her behaviour through her children's eyes.

When Cindy called her sister to speak to her about this upset, her sister reminded her of how their mom's behaviour was during their childhood. Cindy's mom was a perfectionist who didn't play with her children. She made it very clear that she had too many responsibilities as a mother to spend time playing with the children. Cindy and her sister only saw their mother perform tasks and perform them very well. They were very well taken care of but left alone to play together, without their mother.

Thankful for that conversation with her sister, Cindy decided to dig even deeper into her self to uncover why her thoughts and feelings became so negative around household responsibilities. She uncovered that she had an enormous amount of guilt and resentment each time she took care of the duties because she wanted her time to be with the children. She remembered feeling very lonely as a child and wishing desperately for her mother to play with her. She never wanted her two children to feel that way. Therefore, she resented how the duties had to take her away from her children. That anger, resentment and guilt was totally stealing the happiness away from her and her children.

After being aware of this pattern and understanding where it was coming from, Cindy made a choice to think differently. She hired a housecleaner to take care of the majority of the work and she did the day to day chores either after the kids were in bed or she'd make them a game during the day. Dishes became something princesses do to get their nails cleaned before being painted, and making the bed became more fun as they hid special pictures under the mattress to find the next time. Household chores were now fun and Cindy included her children in the game, unlike her mother.

Cindy's mother cannot be blamed for her actions. Instead, it's only about awareness. Awareness of where Cindy's actions were stemming from. Which thoughts and feelings were creating the actions? Then Cindy learnt how to let go of the negativity. If Cindy hadn't self-discovered, her thoughts and feelings would have caused an imbalance in the chakra system and then ultimately, she would have experienced some form of physical ailment due to the constant negativity in the body. Congratulations to Cindy for her ability to self-discover and make the changes!

Here's an analogy that I love to use when speaking about awareness.

Let's use a goldfish – representing us – living in a fish tank – representing our environment, to show us how our negativity becomes buried and can lead to destruction over time.

Picture a goldfish swimming in an aquarium. Over time, his waste settles to the bottom of the tank and becomes buried by colourful little pebbles. The waste is hardly noticeable, but it exists. The fish swims around day after day thinking that its tank is clear and clean, but slowly it becomes a little murky and dirty, smelling from the hidden waste. Then one day it's time for a change. A powerful being from above pours crystal clear water into the tank. Bits of waste work their way out from under the pebbles and into the fish's water, clouding its view. The fish panics. Out of fear, it doesn't move. The comfort of recognizing where it lives and swims every day doesn't exist anymore. The fish closes its eyes tightly, waiting for his fear to disappear. Finally, the fish gains some courage and opens one eye. The tank is clearer. Fresh water is still flowing into the tank. Now with less waste, the fish can breathe better, swim freer, and see further. The fish now realizes that he doesn't need this old waste in his tank and feels better without it.

We are like the fish and his tank. Over time our old core beliefs, negative thought patterns and feelings become buried deep inside us. We exist day to day, thinking we are ok but knowing that we're not as happy as we could be. We decide to ask the spiritual world for help. Once we've asked for help and opened the door for change, help floods in. Overwhelmingly, past experiences come to the surface and we panic. Physical, mental and emotional upheavals are now a regular part of our day. We don't know whom we are anymore, or in which direction to turn. Instead of doing the healing work, we choose to mask the pain with pharmaceutical drugs, staying inside, cutting out friends and more. We close our eyes and turn our back to the pain believing it doesn't exist.

Changing core beliefs and finding your true authenticity takes time, patience, courage, and sometimes physical, mental or emotional pain. A clearer view helps us see which beliefs, thoughts and feelings we'd like to keep and which ones we should let flow away.

The key is to trust in the healing process. Once we do, the spirit world will be happy to help us release negativity from our body, mind and soul. If we don't deal with the issues, but decide to bury them away, our health will deteriorate. We will be unhappy in our tank.

Life will always contain some degree of chaos. Choose to close your eyes in fear or trust that you'll find your way through the fear to happiness. There are always experienced people available to help you, or family and friends who'll be there for you because they love you. The choice of direction is yours once again. I don't judge your path. I just hope you have the courage of the fish to "just keep swimming" as Dori from the movie Finding Nemo said.

When beginning to become aware of your physical, mental, emotional, and spiritual health, you need to understand the chakra system so that you can work through the healing process one step at a time. To try to change or heal everything at once can be a very painful experience but taking small steps will lead to greater success every day. Remember you are painting your life picture. Have patience as you work with each colour of the rainbow.

Chakras:

Let me explain chakras, as a large section of this book relates to each chakra energy center and one of the seven colours of the rainbow associated with it.

The word chakra (or as it is spelled in Sanskrit – Çakra – with the c pronounced as ch) means spinning wheel of energy, and originally referred to a chariot wheel. Later it became associated with the term "wheel of light," which is the modern usage of the word. The seven chakras were first described nearly 2600 years ago, in the ancient sacred texts. Most of the current Western knowledge of the chakra colours comes from an English translation of Sanskrit texts from the 10th and 16th centuries.

We are all made up of 7 different chakras running up and down our spine, constantly spinning. Interestingly, the frequency or vibrancy of these chakras correspond to the frequency of the 7 colours of the rainbow. When measured, a red coloured light vibrates slow and warm – exactly like our bottom root chakra up to violet's frequency with a cool and fast vibration – just like our top crown chakra. It's quite fascinating. You may have heard about chakras if you take yoga, thai chi, reiki, nia, or if you've been to an alternative health practitioner. These chakras centers are connected to major organs and glands on a physical level but also to our emotional, mental and spiritual levels representing the whole person. If we have disturbances on any of these levels, a chakra's vitality will show an imbalance of over activity or under activity. Let me explain using an example of my reoccurring strep throat that I experienced in the past.

Going back to my story about sexual abuse, I didn't speak about it for years. I never told anyone when it happened for fear of not being believed or from the fear of not wanting to get the boys into trouble. To avoid conflict, I kept quiet about my experiences. Having those fears and concerns of voicing is the **1st stage of illness**. They were negative thoughts and feelings. Over time, my throat chakra would have been spinning slowly as my voice wasn't being used and I wasn't expressing true emotions. **This is the 2nd stage**. Now, as an adult, I wanted to begin speaking in front of an audience about detoxing thoughts. I'd forgiven my abusers and thought I was free and clear of any trouble. Nevertheless, although my thoughts had changed, I still had some work to do to completely clear this issue. My business coach kept working with me to unleash my real story to an audience. I was terrified with this idea. I was worried about judgment, blame and authenticity. Would people believe me? Could I get through telling the story without breaking down emotionally during my talk? Was I really an abuse survivor? I didn't want to be labeled as that and it was hard for me to accept the fact that this really was a big part of my story that molded me into who I am today. With all these thoughts and fears arising I started experiencing a constant sore throat. **This is the 3rd stage of illness**. I suffered with laryngitis many times, losing my voice completely for weeks. Then one summer, I had strep throat 4 times! **This is the 4th stage of illness.** This was crazy! Here I was helping other people detox their thoughts and I had strep throat for the 4th time. I needed to face the truth. This was part of my picture and I needed to display the painting for the world to see. I needed to share my experiences; how I overcame so much negative emotion and found forgiveness. I needed to believe in myself and the advice I'd given to others. After that "awareness" I began telling people why it was so important for *me* to detox my thoughts and how I'd done the work, gone through the process, felt enormous amounts of emotion and had emerged as a cleaner person with less toxic thoughts. That was years ago now and I haven't had another bout of strep throat since! I can only imagine what would have happened if I hadn't heard what my body was telling me. Would I have experienced even worse illness in my throat? Would my heart begin having trouble since I was holding onto such emotion? So much more could have developed. I'm very lucky I was open and aware and only suffered minor throat issues to wake me up. Hopefully, this example explains the four different stages of health when dealing with a negative thought.

When we can become aware *first* and change those negative thoughts and feelings before they transpire into an imbalance in the body, we're taking care of our health on all levels.

In the coming chapters we'll be discussing how chakras work and how they connect to the energy of our thoughts and feelings. Imagine how much healthier and happier you'd be if you caught those imbalances in the 1st or 2nd stage of illness. How would you feel if you could permanently release your fear of failure, your negative inner dialogue, your need for recognition, your need to please others constantly, your addictions, and your hidden denials? Think of the freedom your heart, mind and soul will ultimately feel. Ahhhhh. Now imagine if we can begin working on these issues in a fun way. Yes, I said *fun*! Wouldn't that make the process so much better? Of course! So let's use the 7 colours of the rainbow to help us become aware, heal our chakras, and then ultimately heal our physical, mental, emotional and spiritual well being.

Let's Live Life Colourfully!

We'll use:
Red to release Fear and bring in Passion
Orange to release Expectations and bring in Joy
Yellow to release Judgment and bring in Courage
Green to release Guilt and bring in Balance
Blue to release Excuses and bring in Truth
Indigo to release Blame and bring in Inner Peace
Violet to release Denial and bring in Belief

Are you ready to use colour as *your* tool? Let's have some fun...

LIVING IN A COLOURFUL BOX

"We could learn a lot from crayons; some are sharp, some are pretty, some are dull, while others bright; some have weird names, but they all have learned to live together in the same box." Robert Fulghum

Colour caught my attention, the same as every little girl, however I had a real passion about it. I shared a room with my older sister when I was growing up. It was a yellow room with yellow drapes, yellow comforter and yellow wallpaper. It sounds bright and cheery, but I despised it. Yellow was the colour my sister wanted – and needed – but it was *not* the colour for me. Yellow stimulated my mind but I already had a busy mind! I disliked that yellow wallpaper so much, I used to secretly pick at it and peel it away from the wall, which eventually got me into trouble. I wanted to rip it all down and have a blue or purple room but I wasn't allowed. Plus, my sister was older so she got to choose. I used to lie in bed at night, wide awake, singing at the top of my lungs until my parents would tell me, "Angela, enough. Quiet down and go to sleep." Now that I understand how yellow stimulates the mind, it was no wonder that I found falling asleep difficult. Years later, we began to change the room and introduced some pink. By the time I was 15, my older brother moved out and I got his room. I chose a soft feminine blue for the walls and the comforter and finally I felt more at home.

My parents rarely decorated with colour. They appreciated the monotones and the earthly feel. Living in a house without much colour, I found my fix in other ways, such as colouring with 64 different coloured crayons, using coloured chalk outside to make hopscotch grids, owning clothing and jewellery in many colours, and buying binders for school in every colour.

By the time I moved into my own apartment with my new husband, I went crazy using colour. I think my landlord was scared to death when he saw my purple and blue room with the blue ceiling, but I promised him I'd paint it white again when we moved out and then he calmed down and agreed.

When I opened my store, called Heaven & Earth Inc., in Newmarket, Ontario at the age 24, I began my journey of learning and understanding about the powerful effects colour has on our life. I began selling colour therapy products, such as coloured bath products. These change the colour of your bath water and are like food for the soul. I found information about colour therapy and started carrying other products such as candles, clothing and jewellery. I always knew that I loved colour and needed certain colours in my life but I was amazed at the psychological effect it has on our physical, mental, emotional, and spiritual life.

This was a new beginning for me. It marked the beginning of me becoming a Colour Therapist and using colour as my tool for helping people dress, decorate, market their business, and heal their lives.

Now, as a Personal Development Expert and Colour Therapist helping people to change their thought patterns, find their authenticity, and heal their lives, I'm excited to explain colour to you in simple terms so that you'll begin to see colour in a new light.

Let's discuss the history of colour so you can understand how and why it has been used for centuries. As far back as 5,000 years ago, it has been documented that colour feeds and balances the body, mind, and spirit. The seven colours of the rainbow come from light frequencies and light is a natural source of energy. These rainbow colours, with their different frequencies, can make us feel relaxed and calm or make us energetic and stimulated. Although we constantly absorb "colour energy" through our eyes and skin, we also absorb this light through a system of seven energy centers called "Chakras".

Through colour we receive all the energies we need in order to maintain a healthy body, mind, and soul. The National Institute of Mental Health has done studies showing that our mental health, behaviour, and general efficiency in life depends to a great extent on normal colour balance. When something goes wrong, or is out of balance, we can strengthen our energy centers through the conscious use of colour therapy. Colour Energy exists everywhere and can be acquired through the food we eat, the clothes we wear, our surroundings, aromatherapy, sound, gemstones, and bath products, which are all ideal for rebalancing the seven chakras. As consumers, we've been marketed to with colour for years. There are reasons why "For Sales" signs are red and fast food restaurants use red/orange/yellow in their logos. Even hospitals use green and/or blue to induce healing. Researching colour for business purposes is a multi-million dollar industry. We, as consumers, however, don't realize that we're influenced by the colour of products every day.

The seven energy chakras we will be discussing are the root, spleen, solar plexus, heart, throat, brow, and crown chakras. This relates to the colours Red, Orange, Yellow, Green, Blue, Indigo and Violet. It's interesting to note that the seven chakras described so long ago actually have a basis in anatomy – they correspond to five main nerve ganglia of the spinal column and two areas of the brain (upper and lower). So in effect, in accordance with the chakra definition, they truly are "energy centers!"

If we have one or more of these chakra centers out of balance by spinning too quickly or slowly, then over time this can lead to physical, emotional or mental disease. Keeping our seven chakras aligned and working together will lead to a sense of health and balance, which can improve our lives on many different levels. For example, our heart chakra represents a balance of love, trust, and nurturing. If our heart chakra is unbalanced, then we may have difficulty forming good relationships with our loved ones, or it may leave us feeling little empathy for our fellow humans. Or, on the other hand, we may be *too* emotional, and take things too much to "heart", which can lead to unnecessary suffering and worry. There's also some medical evidence that people who live happy lives have a decreased incidence of coronary heart disease, thus showing that a happy heart is a healthier heart! Understanding the relationships between our subtle bodies and our physical bodies can help us to lead happier and healthier lives.

Some people believe that colour therapy is craziness, hog wash or even just a trend. That us practitioners are making this up. Interestingly, many, many different forms of alternative health therapies have been used for centuries for healing on all levels. Hundreds, even thousands of years ago – before pharmaceuticals entered our lives, the people of this earth found natural ways to heal our body, mind and soul. Now, although we're blessed with modern medicine and it's benefits, people are once again searching for alternative health care. Whether it's for preventative reasons or to assist in treating an ailment, we can learn from the teachings of the generations before us.

There are many modalities in alternative health care that I love and support. Aromatherapy, magnetic therapy, sound therapy, and hypnotherapy are just a few. However, my passion is colour therapy! How can you not love colour? Our world is filled with colour, from the bursting colourful flowers to the greenest trees and the bluest turquoise waters. Colour penetrates us, influences our moods, and shows up every day in how we paint our homes to what clothes we choose to wear, and even what foods we eat.

Energy Exercise – You Can Try This Right Now!

Put your hands about 6cm apart facing each other as though you are holding a large glass of water with your hands on either side of the glass. Allow your hands to remain there for at least 1 minute. Sometimes this takes a few minutes and sometimes only a few seconds but you may experience a sensation on your palms and fingers. It may be tingling, it may be pins and needles, you may feel heat, or as though two magnets are repelling. This is your energy. Once you become more in tune to your energy, you may even see the colours dancing between your hands!

Please remember, have no expectations and allow no negative thoughts into your mind. These sensations may not happen right away and that's ok. You're beginning to tap into your own energy after all these years of living! Play with the exercise. Experiment with it at different times of the day. Enjoy the process and have fun feeling your own energy!

HISTORY OF COLOUR AND THE CHAKRAS

"No man is free who is not a master of himself." Epictetus

Before we begin the meanings of colour, you need to understand the history and philosophy of colour. Some of you may be thinking with excitement or despair, "Oh great – history!" but it's important to know where this therapy originated before we decide *why* we need to use it and how to use colour in our lives.

Several findings indicate that colour and light have been used for health treatments since the beginning of recorded time. As far back as 5,000 years ago, it has been documented that colour feeds and balances the body, mind, and spirit. I wanted to share with you some examples of how our ancestors used colour thousands of years ago. If we're going to talk about how colour is healing, it's important to understand how it was used to heal people many, many years ago.

Egypt

Colour was used symbolically by the Egyptians. Many different forms of textures, gemstones and keepsakes were found in Egyptian tombs displaying vibrant colours. Egyptians associated green with fertility and life, black for grief, and yellow for eternity. In writing they used only red and black. Red was used to make the text stand out, such as headings, and account totals, and they also considered red to be unlucky. Ancient Egyptians built solarium-type rooms for ill people, which could be fitted with coloured panes of glass. The sun would shine through the glass and flood the patient with colour.

China

In traditional Chinese medicine, each organ is associated with a colour. This knowledge has been continued today. A biofeedback system that I owned for years analyzed 44 different organs in the body and associated a colour with each organ so that the client and I could see how the organs were functioning.

Greece

Ancient Greeks built healing temples of light and colour. Look at pictures of Greece today and notice how much they paint using the brilliant shades of blue and white. These two colour represent their flag, their Goddess Athena, and the blue sea. Their flowers are usually in beautiful fushia pink. The colours are amazing.

India

The system of colour therapy has prospered in India in the last 50 years. However, colour therapy is rooted in ayurvedic medicine, an ancient form of medicine practiced in India for thousands of years.

Europe

In Europe and the U.S., interest in the therapeutic use of colour developed during the second half of the nineteenth century.

As late as the nineteenth century, European smallpox victims and their sickrooms were draped with red cloth to draw the disease away from the body.

During the early twentieth century, investigations into the therapeutic uses of colour in Europe were carried out, notably, by Rudolph Steiner who related colour to form, shape, and sound. In the schools inspired by Steiner's work, classrooms are painted and textured to correspond to the 'mood' of children at various stages of their development.

US

U.S. Dr. Harry Riley Spitler found that he could produce profound physiological and psychological changes in his patients by altering the colour of light entering their eyes.

So, as you can see, colour therapy has been used for centuries all over the world.

This chakra system, meaning "wheel of energy" really is an incredible creation. It's what ties the physical, mental, emotional, and spiritual elements together to make us the unique, magnificent creation we are in the world. It's absolutely amazing that each chakra center has the same frequency as a colour of the rainbow. Let's understand how they each represent an integral part of our make-up.

Our 7 chakras can be divided into a Physical, Mental, Emotional and Spiritual category for easier understanding.

Physical Chakras – Red Root and Orange Sacral

These bottom two chakras are connected to our physical wellbeing. The first chakra is the Root Chakra, vibrating at the same frequency as the colour red. The second chakra or Sacral Chakra is located above the Red Root, which vibrates as the same frequency as the colour orange.

The Red Root is all about our "roots" – just like a tree. It connects us to our root family. It's the foundation in our lives and the structure. It helps us keep our feet on the ground and bring our dreams into reality. It connects us to our physical health, our immune system, and our blood, spinal column, bones and teeth. If we were having trouble in one of these areas, we may experience immune dysfunctions, such as Chronic Fatigue Syndrome, Fibromyalgia or Arthritis. We can also encounter blood disorders, vitamin and mineral deficiency, and head injuries from having our "head in the clouds". The Red Root is a part of our physical energy center as it's a focus on action and passion.

The Orange Sacral is also part of the physical centers but it's more concerned with the physical act of being playful. It reminds us to be present in the moment and enjoy all that life has to offer. As adults we sometimes forget to play. This energy center helps us to remember that play is an important part of our lives. In visual relation to a tree, it's the bottom of the trunk – the part that we can wrap our arms around and hug. Our Orange Sacral connects us to our femininity or masculinity. It's connected to our sexual reproduction. If it's out of balance, we may experience infertility, a lack of a sex drive, ovarian cysts, and hormone imbalances for example. That's a good reason to play, remain active, and keep the Orange Sacral Chakra happy.

Mental Chakra – Yellow Solar Plexus

The 3rd chakra is related to our mental wellbeing. It's called the Solar Plexus chakra and it's the same frequency as the colour yellow. This chakra is concerned with our concentration, memory, confidence, self-esteem, and having a positive outlook on life. As it visually relates to the tree, think of this representing the trunk of the tree where the branches begin to grow. The Yellow Solar Plexus Chakra connects us to our digestive system, liver, pancreas, kidneys, gall bladder, and colon. When we try to be in control of life and forget to surrender and release to our internal guidance system (that gut feeling) we can experience problems in these areas. In addition, if we're using our mental self too much by becoming a workaholic, stressing about work, or issues causing a lot of mental energy, we can throw this chakra out of balance and create problems for ourselves. When healthy, we are confident, self-assured, quick to think, and we remember to always see the glass as half full instead of half empty.

Emotional Chakras – Green Heart and Blue Throat

The 4th and 5th chakras are connected to our emotional well being. The 4th chakra is the center of *all.* There are three chakras below and three chakras above. This chakra has the same frequency as the colour green. The Green Heart chakra is the balance of giving and receiving love. It's about balance in life on all levels. The heart chakra is the branches of the tree reaching out to give love as well as receiving the love that the universe has to offer. The Green Heart Chakra is a loving frequency, helping us to find forgiveness, compassion, and kindness in not only others but in ourselves as well. It lets us know that we are love and we are loved. Unfortunately, when we've been hurt, lost trust or have low self-worth, this Green Heart Chakra will suffer. This can lead to problems with our heart, lungs, and breasts. With three chakras above and below this Green Heart Chakra, it's very important to keep it healthy as it's the center. In my past experience, most people with issues in the other six chakras usually have a core problem in the Green Heart Chakra.

The 5th chakra is the Blue Throat chakra representing how well we voice our thoughts, feelings, and authenticity. It's also the colour and chakra related to having a restful sleep, calming stress, anxiety, and experiencing harmony in life. This chakra finds our peace and order, gets us organized, and represents loyalty. All too often, if we're not being authentic with ourselves or others, we will experience throat problems. Being authentic, means honouring our beliefs and values in every situation. Have you ever compromised your beliefs and values or made excuses for them in order to please someone else? If you don't honour yourself and voice your truth, you may experience a sore throat, strep throat, laryngitis or tonsillitis, for example. Your throat chakra wants you to express yourself with love. When we live in authenticity, we honour ourselves and others with love.

Spiritual Chakras – Indigo Brow Chakra and Violet Crown Chakra

Our 6th chakra, the Indigo Brow chakra, has also been called "The Third Eye" chakra as it's our way of seeing into the spiritual realm. This is the chakra that connects us to our intuitive gifts, such as that sense of knowing, the ability to see or hear the other side, and the connection with our spiritual support system. It's also connected to our creative gifts, such as painting, song writing, poetry or story telling. In our example of the tree, this Brow Chakra represents the leaves on the trees. The leaves reach up towards the sun, sprouting from the nutrients that run through the trunk from the roots.

Imagine if the roots and trunk couldn't provide the nutrients to the leaves? The leaves wouldn't sprout and grow. When this chakra is blocked, it causes headaches, migraines, plugged ears and sinuses, vertigo, and blurred vision. When healthy, we are guided to our next step, and the words to express and feel our spiritual support system are with us at all times.

Our 7th chakra, with its beautiful violet colour, represents our connection to a higher Divine source. Regardless of what you choose to call this source, this chakra, when open, allows us to connect to ultimate love, compassion, and kindness. It's our crown chakra on the top of our head allowing for all of the wisdom from source to pour into our being and guide us on our mission in life. It is the fruit of our tree. The life that feeds us, nourishes us, and gives the seeds to start a new tree or life.

Failing to utilize this chakra will result in physical pain, struggle, a lack of direction, and constant negativity. When healthy, we see the beauty in every situation and understand our life purpose.

In the following chapters we will focus on each chakra in greater depth for a more thorough understanding. My purpose is to develop your awareness. By aligning your awareness with a colour and chakra center, you will find it easier to understand and heal on your journey. In addition, a positive and negative word for each chakra center has been included to help you easily identify your strong and weak areas.

Kathy House

RED ROOT CHAKRA
PASSION VERSUS FEAR

*"There is no passion to be found playing small - in settling for a life
that is less than the one you are capable of living."*
Nelson Mandela

Have you ever noticed how fear stops you in your tracks and
paralyzes you? When you experience fear you can't move. Think
back to a time when you felt fearful. Maybe it was watching a scary
movie and you covered your eyes with both hands, completely still
as you waited for the fear to stop. It's a painful experience.

We've all gone through experiencing forms of fear. Some more than
others. For now, however, look at where fear is paralyzing you in
other parts of your normal existence. For example, are you fearful of
change? Does leaving your job to go back to school scare the crap
out of you? Are you delaying leaving your spouse after years of
unhappy marriage due to the fear of being alone? Are you fearful of
walking alone at night incase someone is hiding behind the bushes
waiting to attack you?

Well, you're not alone. Fear exists in everyone's world. So much so
that the media plays on our fears everyday. The news, which airs
usually at 12pm, 6pm, and 11pm –three times per day – or CNN
24/7, plays on our fears and negativity. It's always about who was
shot, killed, stabbed, raped, and kidnapped. We've decided to believe
in the fear thinking this is the only way to live. But in doing so, we

stop living our lives with passion. We're surrounded by negative influences every day and we can choose whether or not to be a part of that existence. You can choose to not watch the news. If something really important happens, like 9/11, I'll hear about it on the radio or from neighbours and then I can choose if I want to watch the footage on TV. There are some of us, however, who live in a negative space all the time and enjoy seeking out other negative forces, such as the news, to show them that life *can* be that bad! It always feels better if someone else's life is worse than ours, right?

Imagine if we eliminated the thought of fear and all we had was passion. Passion to live life to the fullest. Passion to follow our dreams. Passion in our relationships. Passion in our careers. Imagine if fear never existed. We'd never be paralyzed. We never stop moving. You see, the opposite of fear is passion. Passion takes action. Passion makes you move. The German poet Hebbel stated, "Nothing great in the world has ever been accomplished without passion."

Think about when you accomplished something great in your life. It may have been knitting your first scarf. Maybe it was achieving 100% in an exam. Maybe it was experiencing the best vacation of your life. Each experience needed passion to achieve it. If fear had crept in, it would never have been accomplished.

Would you like to know an easy way to identify fear? It's the "What If's" in our lives. See if this sounds like you. "What if I can't knit very well and my friend laughs at me?" "What if I fail my exam and I never make it to university?" "What if I travel to another country and become lost and scared?" "What if I never find a partner?" "What if my in-laws show up before my house is cleaned?" What if, what if, what if. It can consume our thoughts. Negative thoughts can and will stop us from living in the moment, taking action, and experiencing passion.

Life always involves movement. That movement can take shape with physical, mental, emotional or spiritual movement. Regardless, movement exists and it's a healthy part of our existence. If we don't move, we become stuck in life and feelings of fear, despair, and insecurity become present. If you're waiting or hoping for something to come into your life in order to feel passionate again, you must take action and create movement. If you want to meet your life partner, get off the couch and go out into the world. Join a book club, sign up for dance lessons, or attend a networking meeting. If you're lacking passion in your career, it's time to create movement. Take a new course or volunteer in a field you're passionate about. Begin to make changes. Positive changes will result in positive experiences. Movement keeps the body and our chakras flowing, which results in a healthier life. Fear of movement will keep you stagnant and slowly break down your physical body. Colds, flus, immune dysfunctions, teeth problems, fatigue, and weak bones can all manifest when our Root Chakra is out of balance with fear in our lives. We need to stay healthy to move through life and live with passion. Where do you need to create passion in your life? Passion takes action!

I'll share a great example of a person to whom I'm very close with. For privacy purposes, I will call her Mary.

Mary lives a full life as a mother, nurturer, and friend to many. She was married, but not happily. She kept moving forward in life trying to heal her marriage while continuing to be involved in her children's upbringing, her church, volunteering, and more. Slowly, Mary started to become ill. She was sleeping hours upon hours per day. Her body constantly ached. She felt depressed and anxious, and she began to feel very alone.

With the medical industry not able to physically help her, Mary began to seek alternative methods of healing. Through her research and health contacts, she began to become aware of how her thoughts and feelings were negative and fear based. She began to see a link connected to her physical body. She totally feared leaving her marriage. Being a stay-at-home mom her whole life she felt as though she had no skills to obtain work. The thought of providing for herself and her children scared her. Mary also feared her husband's behaviour knowing that her leaving may cause even more upset and conflict in the marriage. Mary felt trapped and stuck in an unhappy and unhealthy marriage.

Through the years, while still suffering with illness, Mary began to create passion in her life. She went back to school and became a teacher. She gained confidence, made new friends, and started having movement in her life. Finally, she overcame her fear and left her husband. Although she moved through difficult times, Mary finally found happiness. She's now remarried, living in the country surrounded by nature, has healed many aspects of her body, and has found passion again in her life.

Mary is a great example of how long term fear can create physical root chakra disability. We are not all able to conquer fear in a day or week. Sometimes it takes longer – even years. However, working through fear and creating movement creates action and passion!

Challenge:

I challenge you to experience the colour red to bring in the passion. Use red in your clothing, your home décor, eat more red foods, write with a red pen, and wear a red gemstone, such as a Tiger's Eye or Jasper. Now write down what passion you want to attract into your life. Next write down a fear and all of your "What If" statements pertaining to that passion. How many "What If" statements do you have? How much are they keeping you from taking action and finding a passion? How do these fears relate to old thought patterns and belief systems? Are you willing to let go of these fears? Change your thoughts around them by writing new affirmations to support your passion. How can you use red to support you in this direction?

Here's an example:

Passion: I want to go back to school and receive my degree.

Fear: I won't complete the course. It will take too much time, energy, and money to invest.

What Ifs:

- What if I can't remember the material for the exam?
- What if I don't have time to study while being a parent?
- What if my family laughs at me for doing this in my 40's?
- What if I never find a job in my new area of expertise because I'm too old?
- What if it is too expensive and I can't afford it?

Old Beliefs:

- I should have got my degree when I was young.
- I should have gone to school before having kids, not the other way around.
- If I mess this up, I'll look like a failure.

New Affirmations:

- I am never too old to learn new things.
- I can accomplish anything I set my mind to.
- I am a great role model for my children.
- I am courageous for trying something new.
- I am attracting money in expected and unexpected ways.
- I am honouring my passion in life.

Bring RED into your life to support the Root Chakra:

- Use a red binder at school
- Wear red underwear every day
- Eat red apples and drink red cranberry juice each morning
- Listen to music with good bass and drums. Rock and blues are great
- Drum with my hand drum
- Walk barefoot through grass to connect to mother earth

Wear our RED Garnet gemstone angel pendant

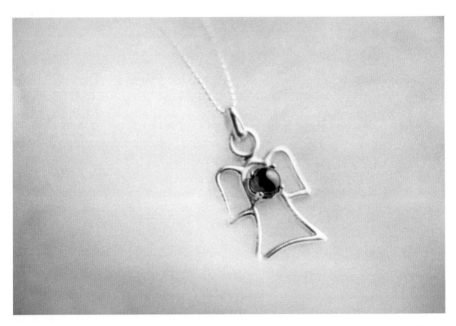

NAVID BAKTASH

ORANGE SACRAL CHAKRA
JOY VERSUS EXPECTATIONS

"We are shaped by our thoughts; we become what we think. When the mind is pure, joy follows like a shadow that never leaves."
Buddha

Having expectations in life seems to be a natural trait for us humans. Most of the time we don't even realize that we are suffering with expectations, let alone high ones. We place expectations on others frequently. We expect people to show up on time. We expect them to remember our birthday. We expect them to know how to follow our routine, when in reality, each person has their own thoughts, feelings, belief systems and values, which determines their reactions. We fail to realize that if we don't voice our expectations, most people won't know what they are and fail to live up to them, thereby disappointing us. This steals our joy. If we're enjoying our birthday with family and friends and we "expect" a friend to arrive for dinner and they don't show up, usually our thoughts will focus on the fact that the friend isn't there and we lose the joy that we've been experiencing. Our thoughts create our happiness and we choose to kill our joy with these expectations.

Expectations placed upon ourselves are very detrimental as we usually set our sights too high to achieve our desired outcome. We always want to do our best, perform our best, and succeed beyond our dreams but sometimes we set our goals so high that we can't help but fail, and unfortunately, this kills our joy.

For example, I had a client who was an avid golfer. He used to golf three times per week. Hearing how much he golfed, a usual assumption would be that he loved the game of golf and enjoyed it immensely. Unfortunately, over the years, his love of the game disappeared due to his high expectations of the outcome of each game. For those non-golfers, a lower score is better as there are less strokes (or swings) in order to get the ball onto the green and into a hole. This man had it in his head that he *had* to get a great score of 70, in an 18-hole course, in order to have fun and succeed in the game. Every time he reached a new hole, he'd have a high expectation of the outcome. He wasn't focused on the beautiful greenery, the gorgeous view, the perfect weather, the friends and colleagues he was with for the day, or the pure joy of enjoying the game of golf. Instead, all he could think about was his expectation of reaching his goal. Unfortunately, each time he played he was frustrated and he beat himself up for not reaching his expectations. He lost his joy for the game.

I'm not suggesting that we shouldn't have goals. I'm suggesting that we create obtainable goals and take steps to achieve them one by one. If my client had rewarded himself for a good game and enjoyed the process of continuously getting a little bit better, he would have maintained the joy and his sacral chakra would be spinning in a healthy manner. Instead he put so much pressure on himself to reach 70, that he lost sight of the joy in the game. Interestingly, my client came to see me for counseling as his marriage was falling apart and he had lost his sex drive. He wasn't finding life fun anymore and he wanted to know how to change that. His 2nd chakra was blocked. The Orange Sacral chakra is all about joy and living in the present moment. It also connects us to our physical well being and our relationships. It didn't surprise me that my client was experiencing marital trouble and a low sex drive. His Orange Sacral chakra was blocked due to all of his expectations. He had expectations not only in his golf game, but at work, with his employees, and definitely at home with his wife and children. I explained to him that we can't place the expectation that his marriage would be fixed in a month, and we worked on eliminating the small expectations step by step in order to bring in more joy. Over time he began to smile more, let go of stress at home and at work, spend more time playing with his children, and eventually the marriage healed.

The Orange Sacral Chakra reminds us to play and enjoy life. It's a natural part of being a child but, as adults, we forget to maintain this important value. We forget to play. Children don't have expectations when they play. They don't say, "I'm going to do a perfect canon ball into this pool." Instead they say, "Watch *this* canon ball!" and however it turns out, they have fun in the moment. For a healthy 2nd chakra, remember to be present in the moment and experience the joy in each situation. It's so easy for adults to think about our responsibilities, duties, and what needs to be accomplished instead of focusing on what's happening in the present moment. Children are a great reminder for us to just *be* and experience joy.

Challenge:

Write in a journal, where in your life are you *not* living in the present moment?

When someone talks to you or needs you, are you 100% there for them or are you thinking about other responsibilities?

What high expectations do you place on your friends?

What high expectations do you place on your partner?

What high expectations do you place on your children?

What high expectations do you place on *you*?

How can you experience *joy* today?

Bring ORANGE into your life to support the Sacral Chakra:

- Eat oranges and drink orange juice
- Spread a big orange blanket out in nature for a picnic
- Listen to fun music and dance (2nd chakra likes playful movement)
- Go to a comedy club and laugh
- Create a fun date night with your partner
- Hang out with a child and use your imagination – finger paint

Wear our ORANGE Carnelian gemstone angel pendant

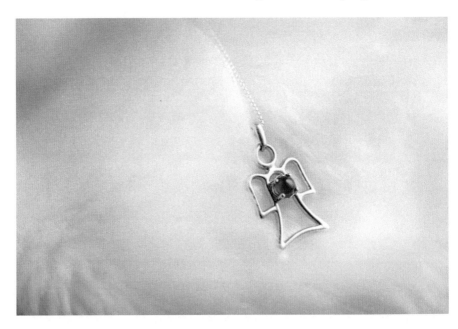

NAVID BAKTASH

YELLOW SOLAR PLEXUS
JUDGMENT VERSUS POSITIVITY

As we enter into the Solar Plexus Yellow chakra, we are brought to the frequency that represents our mental state. Our mind is constantly working. According to research reported by Dr. Dennis Gersten, a diplomat of the American Board of Psychiatry and Neurology, the average person has approximately 15,000 thoughts per day. Can you remember all 15,000 thoughts you've had today? I'm guessing not. However, of all the details that you can remember, how many of those thoughts were mainly focused in one direction? Were you constantly replaying a conversation in your head? Were you focused on your chores for the day and what you needed to accomplish? Were you experiencing happy memories of the birthday party your partner threw for you last night? Take a moment and try to pinpoint how your thought process has been functioning. Now with this awareness, see if your thoughts have been more negative or positive throughout this day. The answer may surprise you!

Most of the time we're not consciously aware of our thought patterns. The majority of us are thinking these 15,000 thoughts every day without any awareness. Unfortunately, those nasty, negative thoughts can sneak into our mind and sometimes monopolize our day, which ultimately leads to dis-ease in our body when not corrected. By the time we actually voice a negative thought, we have already thought about this 100 times in our head!

So when you state, "I'm too ugly," you would have already thought that statement 100 or more times in your head before you voiced it as a reality.

When this happens, we need to have the yellow frequency of Courage to look inside ourselves, own what we are thinking, and begin to make the necessary changes. Believe it or not, this takes a great deal of courage. It's very easy for us to be consumed by the negative side of our mental chakra, which is all about judgment. Without even realizing we're doing it, we judge others and ourselves and hold those thought patterns in our Solar Plexus chakra.

Deepak Chopra states in his book, *The Seven Laws of Spiritual Success* to try not to judge for a mere 30 seconds in your day. When I first heard this, I laughed out loud, immediately judging the statement. I thought it was a misprint in the book. I said, "Thirty seconds! That can't be right. I'll try 30 minutes or 3 hours." Needless to say Deepak *did* mean 30 seconds and I experienced this firsthand. One day while walking along the historic shopping district in my home town I was criticizing the store windows thinking that they could be displayed much better. I wondered why the store owners didn't try harder or make their windows more appealing when it was a tourist area. Then, I was watching people walk by on the street and passed a young girl. I wondered how anyone could wear such tight jeans when their body shape didn't match the look. All of a sudden, I stopped walking and turned inward towards my thoughts. I had an incredible awareness of how I was judging everyone and everything and it didn't stop throughout my whole walk. That meant 30 seconds of non-judging was very difficult for me and Deepak had been right. I was stunned. I had no idea my mind was constantly playing this negative game. After this awareness and realizing I had no right to judge anyone or anything, I began to dig deeper into my personal mental state. Unfortunately, I found myself judging myself too frequently. I easily called myself names and put myself down when I didn't do a task right or forgot to do something simple. In addition, I beat myself up physically, as many women do, thinking that we're not good enough, smart enough, beautiful enough, loving enough, and so on. when in truth that's false information. Here I was, every day judging myself and others. Thank goodness for this awareness and thank you Deepak Chopra, because due to this experience, I let go of a ton of judgment and started living in truth and love. Judgment still sneaks in from time to time but I can catch myself and my thoughts much quicker than I could years ago and my health has improved dramatically in my solar plexus as a result. I used to suffer with irritable bowel syndrome, food sensitivities, and even had gall bladder surgery. These are all connected to the Solar Plexus and the mental self. Now I'm happy to say those issues are obsolete from healing my own journey through self-discovery.

Challenge:

While using the colour Yellow through clothing and foods to help you through this process, I want you to find an accountability partner to support you and make you aware of when you speak a negative thought. It should be your spouse, an adult, a friend, or someone you see or talk to frequently. Every time you voice a negative thought, have your friend say to you, "Say that again". For example, if you say, "I never get anything right" I want your accountability partner to say, "Say that again". This is *not* to have you say it again. This act will help you recognize *when* you say this statement and *how often*. Do not judge yourself or beat yourself up for voicing this statement. It's for awareness only. In a short time, you'll notice that you can catch yourself thinking it before you speak it. You then have the opportunity to replace the statement with a positive statement, such as "I'm always learning." Eventually, you'll *not* say or think anything negative at all. Instead, you'll focus on the positive side of your mental state and say, "I'm always learning" and then you'll feel much better on the inside. Your Solar Plexus chakra will thank you.

Bring YELLOW into your life to support the Solar Plexus:

- Wear a yellow dress or tie
- Eat lemons, grapefruits, pineapple, honey, and yellow peppers
- Play classical music or listen to music from around the world to stimulate the mind
- Write positive affirmations down on yellow post it notes and place them around your house
- Buy a positive self-help book and highlight your favourite quotes in a yellow highlighter pen

Wear our YELLOW Citrine gemstone angel pendant

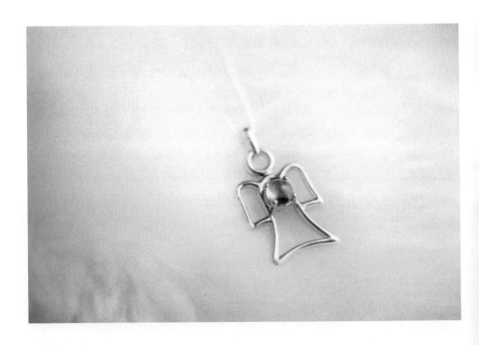

VICKIE SPARKS

GREEN HEART CHAKRA
BALANCE VERSUS GUILT

"Don't run around and try to heal all of your friends.
Do your own mental work and heal yourself.
This will do more good for those around you than anything else."
Louise Hay

The heart chakra, represented by the colour green, sits smack in the middle of all of our chakras. It's the center point of our energy systems. There are three chakras above and three chakras below this point. Therefore, the heart chakra represents balance between the chakras as well as balance in our lives. It's also connected to our emotional wellbeing.

In a time in our lives where being busy seems to have become the norm, this green chakra reminds us to find balance in life for our physical, mental, emotional and spiritual state. How well are you taking care of yourself on all these levels? So often we see someone who is fantastic at taking care of their physical body but may not be able to express emotions. Or you may know someone who meditates and connects to spirit every day but fails to incorporate their mission on earth. This chakra reminds us that life is about balance. Every day check in with yourself to see if you've taken care of your physical body, your mental state, your emotional state, and taken time to connect to your spiritual power. When we use all elements together every day, we will have a health body, mind, and soul.

After having thousands of clients over the years, who are mainly women, I've learned that the greatest way women neglect balance in their lives is with the balancing of giving and receiving love. All too often I've met women who are the biggest givers in the world. They give their time, energy, money, compassion, empathy, and love to their families, friends, career, co-workers, schools, charities and more. While giving out of love is a beautiful trait to have, it's only beautiful when the giver also *receives* time, energy, money, compassion, empathy, love, and more from the people in their lives. In order to give love, you must also be able to receive it. I like to think of our heart chakra as our gas tank and our body as our car. God gave you a physical body as your car to drive your spirit around while learning and living in life. When you continuously drive your car, your gas tank runs out of fuel. How can your car function without gas? It can't. If you try, your car will start to break down and finally stop working just like your body. If you give, give, give (just like drive, drive, drive) your body will be out of balance and your gas tank (heart chakra) will run out of fuel (energy). Eventually, your body will tell you that there's no balance in your life and illness will prevail if don't listen to the signs.

I've seen this over and over again with the women I meet. Men, I know you're out there too! However, 95% of my clientele has been women. Have you ever gone out for a coffee or tea with a friend and tried to pay the bill only to have the friend shove their money in front of you so they can treat you instead? They find it so difficult to accept the fact that you're treating them to a coffee as a random act of kindness. Then, when you do pay, they feel guilty! Now instead of a $2 cup of coffee being a treat it has become a guilt fest. The person treating (or giving) feels bad and frustrated and the person receiving feels guilty. That's a lose-lose situation. To make this a win-win situation, the receiver needs to accept the kindness and love and simply say thank you to their giver of love. By receiving the kindness, the giver feels great in their heart for doing a random act of kindness and treating their friend, and the receiver opens their heart by saying thank you and receives the love. How beautiful is that situation?

I bet you know someone right now who has difficulty receiving kindness. Are you one of them? Take a moment to think about all the things in life you would love to receive. Maybe a new car, a change in career, attract a soulmate, travel to an exotic place, buy a new television…whatever! I'll promise you right now that you will never receive these gifts if you cannot receive a $2 cup of coffee from a friend. How is the universe going to provide you with amazing gifts and opportunities if you have difficulty accepting a $2 cup of coffee? It's impossible as the universe works with positive thoughts and feelings only, not negative. It's the law of attraction.

The Heart Chakra is crucial in our health. A blockage in this chakra caused by guilt and resentment can kill. Actually, any imbalance of energy will, over time, cause ill effects. My concern for women specifically, is that the majority of us have difficulty in this heart chakra in balancing the giving and receiving love. Unfortunately, it can cause heart palpitations, high blood pressure, and even breast cancer.

The core of the heart chakra issue is a lack of self-worth and self-love. When we have difficulty receiving, are we really saying that we don't 'deserve' to receive? Or if we do, we feel enormous amounts of guilt. Somehow in life, we've been brought up to believe – especially as women – that it's selfish to receive. I was brought up as a child to believe, "It's better to give than to receive." The problem with this belief is that if someone is giving, someone is receiving. Our lack of self-worth creates a multitude of problems for us in life. It pushes us down instead of raises us up. It makes us hide and shy away from the beautiful person we are inside. After counseling thousands of women over the years, I can honestly say that the #1 issue women have is a lack of self-worth.

When you feel worthy to receive, your life will bring you abundance in all areas.

Do yourself a favour and start giving back to you. It may be in receiving kindness but it also can be in treating yourself well. Take a candlelit bath, go for an afternoon walk in nature, call an old friend and chat, take a course, eat chocolate guilt free. Every time you treat yourself well, your heart chakra's gas tank will fill with more love and you'll be able to give more love to others. As a result, you'll begin to experience self-worth and self-love. Not only is giving and receiving love with others important, but self-love will sky rocket your heart chakra and keep your gas tank full every day!

Challenge:

Begin noticing if you can receive kindness. Start with compliments. When someone gives you a compliment on your hair, your clothing, the great work you've accomplished, say nothing but "thank you!" Watch how your response lights up the other person. Notice how you begin to fill your own gas tank. If compliments are too easy, accept when a friend takes you out for coffee or dinner. Then see how you're accepting gifts in other areas of your life, such as having someone help you house clean, having your neighbour change your tires, or accept a friend's help with babysitting. You'll find that the universe will keep providing you with amazing gifts, opportunities and more when you are able to receive more and more. And don't worry, you'll always have a kind heart to give to others in return.

Bring GREEN into your life to support the Heart Chakra:

- Sleep in green sheets with green pillow cases and green pajamas. It's a fantastic way to absorb green energy. In addition, green eases sore muscles and relaxes the mind so it's a great colour for sleeping and soothing the soul
- Eat green vegetables, such as spinach, kale, green peppers, zucchini, and cucumber
- Walks in nature are also great for green energy. Filling your lungs up with fresh air in nature is a beautiful way to support and energize the heart chakra. Walk barefoot in green grass
- Listen to soft, calming music involving nature sounds. Love songs are great for the heart chakra. Feel and heal

Wear our GREEN Jade gemstone angel pendant

ANGELA DACEY

BLUE THROAT CHAKRA
TRUTH VERSUS EXCUSES

"Life doesn't happen TO me it happens FOR me."
Tony Robbins

Everything in your life has shaped you into who you are today. You have developed core values and core beliefs, which innately connect you to your authenticity. Interestingly, we all have a different collage of values and beliefs yet we are attracted to those people who share similar ones with us.

I personally own the values of freedom, spirituality, and authenticity. Without these top three core values in my life, I wouldn't feel authentically me.

There are many core values to choose from and in my course, Detox Your Thoughts, we explore them all to find your true core values. For now, take a look at these core values and choose your top three.

Security	Creativity	Peace
Loyalty	Respect	Prosperity
Forgiveness	Hope	Fun/Humour
Honour	Authenticity	Love

Are your top three present in your life through your relationships, career or friendships? Where are you avoiding these core values in your life or where are they present?

With the Throat Chakra being connected to an emotional base center, we are called to look into our heart and use our throat – our voice – to express our true authenticity. When we honour our true values and beliefs with love, we are able to express ourselves to the world as authentic, unique individuals.

The Blue Throat Chakra loves truth. It is healthy when we speak the truth and honour our true selves. As soon as we begin making excuses for who we are or what values and beliefs we own, it begins to suffer.

For example, if you chose fun/humour as a top core value but you fail to create fun in your life, how are you honouring yourself? As a child, did you constantly laugh? Were you playing and being free? If you're the type of person who's working all the time, under a lot of stress or has lots of responsibilities, but chose the fun/humour core value, take notice of adding fun into your life. It's who you are! Your true authentic self needs to shine and you need to feed it the food that will make it glow!

Your authentic self will shine by using your voice. We were given a voice for a reason. We are humans who are able to express themselves and voice our authentic self. Communication, the ability to *ask* for help, and to speak with love creates a strong, healthy throat chakra. To make excuses for ourselves and our actions is detrimental. To not ask for help when we are in need will further decrease the positive affects of this chakra.

How many times has a situation occurred where you later thought, "What I really wanted to say was....?" So often we bite our tongue, resisting to speak what we really want to express. When we suppress that voice, we're really hiding who we really, truly are. We usually like to make up excuses as to "why" we didn't voice: "I didn't want to hurt their feelings," "It wasn't the right time," "She wouldn't understand," "There was no time to get into it," "I didn't want him to get into trouble," and so on. Excuses, no matter how relevant they may seem, will block our throat chakra and stop us from voicing the truth and who we really are.

I'm now going to share a personal story with you. Being real and authentic has been a life journey for me. A few years ago I was working with a great business coach who also understood the connection to the spirit world. Considering my business is very spiritually based, I had to have a coach that understood that spiritual language and my soul purpose. During our time together, I was doing a lot of professional speaking. I was teaching people about 'Detoxing Their Thoughts' in a room with 100-200 people every month. I love teaching this information, as I love to have people experience an "aha" moment and change their life from that moment forward. One day during a meeting my coach pushed me deeper into my self to uncover my true story. He wanted to know on a deep level why I chose to teach this information. It was then that I realized for years I'd been saying it was to help heal family members and friends that were suffering with a chronic illness. I believed that it was all about helping them. Interestingly, that was my excuse. In reality, after some soul searching, I realized that it was the process of helping myself. I was one of the women of the world who experienced sexual abuse as a child. When I realized during the meeting that *this* was my true, authentic story, I tried to deny the fact. I didn't want to discuss it and I didn't want to be labeled as the girl who was abused. However, with my coach's help, I'd come to realize that if I was going to talk about being authentic, I needed to own my authenticity. I needed to admit that I'd personally experienced a trauma and had overcome so many thoughts and feelings around this past situation.

Honestly, this scared me to death. To date, I'd told a few friends about the experience but I'd never shared this information in a public setting. I was scheduled to do a talk in the fall. Throughout the entire summer I suffered with strep throat – four times to be exact! I had laryngitis as well. My throat chakra literally closed up from the fear expressing my true authenticity. After trying all alternative health options and taking antibiotics more frequently than I'd wanted to that summer, I finally surrendered to the fact that the imbalance in my body was due to my fear of voicing the truth. Needless to say, awareness is only half the battle because after that realization, my throat problems cleared up.

Nervous, scared, but feeling empowered, I spoke about my experience during that talk in the fall. It took a phenomenal amount of courage. I was sweating from head to toe but I did it. My reward was that some women approached me afterwards thanking me for discussing the topic so openly as they also were survivors of sexual abuse. My talk had helped them to heal.

I felt elated, empowered, free and true to my life purpose. Unfortunately, my family discovered that I was speaking about these experiences in public and due to shame and denial around the topic they made it very clear that it was unacceptable to them. They wanted me to stop speaking my truth immediately. Knowing myself as I do and working through this great trauma and changing people's lives because of it, I couldn't agree to stop my voice. I'd never tell the story in such a way to accuse anyone or hurt anyone. I told the story from a place of forgiveness. However, due to the situation and my strength to continue on my journey of authenticity, I lost contact with my family. It was a terrible experience but mandatory. If I couldn't honour my core value of authenticity, I couldn't honour myself. My story created who I am and it has helped to heal many people, including myself.

This is the power of owning your core values. When they are such a big part of who you are, you have no choice but to honour them. Otherwise, you will always be denying yourself. Authenticity may not be one of your core values. The key is to uncover your values and live by them every day. I take people on this journey of self-discovery in my Intensive Journey of Self Discovery course, Soul Mala. You can view my website for more details.

I like to believe that in life, this earth is a school where we learn, grow, change, and are constantly tested in order to truly test our inner spirit. Learning to voice is one of those challenges.

Some people in life are physically unable to voice. However, they find a way to get their message across. Many phenomenal people have written books, painted pictures, used sign language, and more to express their true self. How well are you expressing you?

Challenge:

Find a simplistic chanting CD and begin a daily ritual of chanting. Become aware of how easy or difficult it is for you to follow the chant and sing out loud. Many of us who have difficulty voicing also have difficulty chanting. It's a great way to determine if an issue lies within the throat chakra. I personally suggest chanting the Sanskrit word OM, which is the sound of universal energy. There are many CDs available, or online downloads that offer a melody and chant for you to follow.

The most amazing thing about chanting is that when you fully release your throat chakra and chant, you will begin to feel the vibration moving inside your body, particularly within one specific chakra center. Different notes on the scale and different sounds will radiate a frequency inside your body and help to open up your chakras and heal them.

Bring BLUE into your life to support the Throat Chakra:

- Begin chanting a simple chant, yet powerful - OM
- Sleeping in blue sheets, pillow cases, and pajamas. Blue is known to induce sleep, help pain, ease headaches, and calm the mind
- Wear a necklace around the throat of Sodalite or Blue Lace Agate to give your throat chakra a burst of energy
- Rub the aromatherapy scent of Melissa on your neck for increased energy
- Wear a blue scarf/tie around your neck to help you speak freely and with love

Wear our BLUE Lapis Lazuli gemstone angel pendant

VICKIE SPARKS

INDIGO BROW CHAKRA
INNER PEACE VERSUS BLAME

"Spiritual growth is like childbirth. You dilate, then you contract. You dilate, then you contract again. As painful as it all feels, it's the necessary rhythm for reaching the ultimate goal of total openness."
Marianne Williamson

We are now moving to the spiritual centers for our chakras. The Indigo Brow Chakra is located in between our eyebrows and for years it has been called the "Third Eye." With the Third Eye we are able to see into the spirit world and into our own inner spirit.

In order to connect with this chakra center and experience the doorway to inner peace, we need to be ok with silence. Also, it's important to work on clearing the negative thoughts and feelings that have been creating toxic energy in our body. Finally, we must trust that we have a support group of loving beings helping us on this journey. Every religion and spiritual belief system supports messengers and guardians in our lives.

Let's start with the first point. Silence.

Did that blank page throw you off your routine? Did you wonder where the words had gone? Did you think there was a misprint in the book and you lost some important information? My intention was to create a feeling of silence in writing. What were your thoughts and feelings for those few seconds?

We are so used to information overload. With technology, the internet, cell phones, media advertising, and so on we're bombarded with information 24/7. Rarely do we experience silence. When we do, we're looking for the next thing to create noise. This is really about blocking our thoughts and feelings and using an escape to mute our inner spirit that's talking to us. There was a time in my life when I had to have the television on in the background or the radio playing constantly if I was home alone. When I began my journey of self-discovery, I began to realize that I couldn't focus on myself with the noise so I started to create silence. However, in that silence, my brain was *loud*. I was constantly thinking, analyzing, critiquing, feeling, wondering, and second guessing. By shutting off the TV and radio, I began to see the dis-ease in my body and listen to what my mind and body were saying. I was no longer ignoring myself, I was acknowledging myself. I gave myself permission to hear myself internally. This was profound. You can't heal what you don't know is there. The silence helped me to find out what needed to be healed. Now I no longer enjoy watching TV. While at a friend's house for a week by myself, I was excited that they had satellite TV since I don't have TV at my house. After flipping through 100 channels and feeling dissatisfied with the content then finally choosing an old show I used to watch, the commercials and noise drove me crazy. Instead, I put on satellite radio and regained my balance.

Second point – clearing negative thoughts and feelings.

I like to use the phrase, "When you clear your (bleep), you clear your channels." We're all able to connect to our inner spirit and our messengers in this life. Just like finding a radio station, sometimes the stations come through clearer than others. When we begin to heal our old thoughts and feelings, we make room for new love and light to enter. Since our angels, guides, messengers, and loved ones work in a frequency of love and light, they can come through to help us in a much clearer way when we remove the old to make room for the new. The more you work on yourself and the more you remove the negative from your life, the more you will connect and notice your spiritual support group every day. In addition, the more you remove the old, outdated thoughts and feelings, the more inner peace you will have within. Although all negative thoughts and feelings create imbalance in our body, the main thought and feeling to affect this energy center of the Brow Chakra is blame. As soon as we blame someone or blame ourselves, our inner peace shuts down. How can we be in a place of inner peace when in our hearts we are blaming people, the world, the government, the environment, jobs, our family, and our friends for our problems. Have you heard the saying, "When you point a finger, there are three fingers pointing back at you?" This is a great example of when you decide someone or something else is the culprit for your problems. You need to really look inside yourself to figure it out, not blame the outside world. In order to achieve inner peace, you must take full responsibility and accountability for your thoughts, feelings, and actions. No one is responsible for them but *you*. No one can "make" you feel a certain way – only you can. When you realize that you're blaming others or yourself for the misgivings in the world, and you begin to look inside for the real truth, then you will find the inner peace you are searching for.

Let me give you an example.

I had a female client who was around 45-years-old. She'd been a stay-at-home mom for years; she was overweight and had a low self-esteem. Now that her kids were grown up and didn't need their mother all the time, she desired to find a passion and go back to work. She loved fashion and wanted to start working in a retail position. She began to hand in resumes to places only to find herself rejected over and over again. Feeling insecure and not wanting to look at herself in the situation, she began blaming her different experiences in life for creating this current problem. She'd tell her husband, "I can't find a job because 'they' never hire stay-at-home moms. If 'you' had been able to make more money, we could have afforded daycare and I would have been able to work and keep up my resume. How am I supposed to find a job now with no experience?" Then she began to blame her parents for her eating habits during her upbringing. She phoned her mother one day and complained, "Mom, I can't get a job in the fashion world because I'm overweight and 'they' don't want an overweight person selling their clothes. If 'you' had been home to make more healthy meals instead of serving us frozen dinners, I wouldn't have this weight problem and I'd be able to get a job."

Can you see how this lady blamed her husband and her mother for her current experiences? She was pointing the finger at both of them instead of taking a look at what needed to be changed inside of her. After a few counseling sessions, she saw that it was her responsibility to keep her skills up while being a mother. Her husband did the best that he could at the time and they'd agreed to have one parent home to raise the children. She especially wanted to do this act of love for her children as her mother had to work throughout her childhood days and couldn't be there much for her children. She came to realize that she had acquired many transferrable skills to add to the workforce. Unfortunately, she was always blaming her husband for her life not working out the way she felt it should. In addition, she realized that she was an adult and in full control of her own eating habits and daily exercise. Although it was true that her mother was a working mother and couldn't always provide a home cooked meal, my client was a stay-at-home mom and had provided herself and her family with healthy alternatives. Once again, by removing the finger pointing and looking internally for old thoughts and feelings to be removed, she felt more confident and made amazing changes in her life. She uncovered her amazing skills and transferred them to a resume in order to find a great job. She was hired immediately. In addition, she took a cooking class in the evening and found new ways to cook with healthy alternatives. She began exercising and she lost weight. Now she's looking and feeling fantastic and she no longer blames her husband and mother for her issues!

Third point – trusting your messengers

Trust and believe that we are a spiritual being in a human body. When we realize that we're spiritual beings living a purpose, we begin to honour ourselves more and trust the signs that appear on a daily basis. How often have you turned on the radio only to find that the words of the song are exactly what you needed to hear? How many times have you looked at the clock to see the same numbers in one day? Have you ever noticed that when you think of a past loved one, you'll suddenly see a butterfly? They're all signs from your messengers that they are with you and there to help you. When you recognize the signs, you will see them more and more. The more you clear yourself of unwanted thoughts and feelings, the more your energy will be aligned with the spiritual support system, and the more you will feel, see, smell, and notice them.

We often wonder if coincidences in life are just coincidences. I believe that it's the universe's way of saying hello but remaining anonymous. Over the years I've found that when we remove our own free will and ask for what we need, our messengers respond immediately. We may not see the results immediately, but we can be guaranteed that they've heard our request and are working on an outcome that serves our highest and greatest good.

Angels and guides can be asked for help every day. They will do everything from assisting you with parking spots, to offering guidance and direction on a tough topic. I've come to have completely trust in my messengers and their presence in my life. It's amazing how much they show themselves to us. We just have to look, listen, acknowledge their presence, and say thank you.

When we become comfortable with silence, when we clear old thoughts and feelings, and when we trust in our spiritual messengers to support us, our connection to our inner spirit and inner peace becomes present in our lives. It's a wonderful awareness and an extraordinary gift. Once you connect to your brow chakra, your life will have new meaning. You'll begin to see the bigger picture and you'll know you're never alone because in the silence lies your greatest gifts.

Challenge:

Be in silence for 30 minutes a day. Start by turning off any noise. Drive in the car without the radio. Turn off the TV. Recognize and write down your thoughts and feelings every day in a journal.

Once you have mastered this exercise, continue the 30 minutes silence every day but now sit in a comfortable position and remain seated in silence for the duration of the time. Once again, listen to your thoughts and tune into your feelings then write them in your journal.

When you feel that you can sit in silence for 30 minutes without your mind racing, focus on your breath. Ask your angels, guides, and loved ones to be with you and ask them to guide you. Ask them what it is you need to know for the day. Then listen. Whatever words come into your head, trust them. Listen to the messages. Feel the feelings and become aware of their presence. They will come only with love. Allow them to show you how to recognize when they are near. It may be with a sign, a whisper, a smell or a feeling. It will be special and perfect for you. When you have completed this task, return to the room and write your experience in your journal. Remember to say thank you. Angels love gratitude!

Bring INDIGO into your life to support the Brow Chakra:

- Sit on an Indigo yoga mat
- Hold an amethyst stone in your hand or in your pocket
- Burn a lavender candle
- Play the beautiful music of Deva Premal (my favourite. She has over 14 CDs)
- Write your findings in an Indigo journal

Wear our INDIGO Iolite gemstone angel pendant

RON CLIFFORD

VIOLET CROWN CHAKRA
BELIEF VERSUS DENIAL

"Alone we can do so little. Together we can do so much."
Helen Keller

This chakra sits on the top of our head as it states itself as the "Crown" chakra. Also a spiritual energy center, this chakra is now bringing the highest Divine love and light into our being. Whereas Indigo represents inner peace, Violet represents outer peace. It doesn't matter the title or label you put on your highest power. I like to call this loving energy "God" because that was the title I grew up with and it feels comfortable to me. However, many others call this higher power Ala, Jah, Krishna, Omnipresent and Divine Source, to name but a few. There's no right and wrong answer.

When I owned my retail store, Heaven & Earth, in Newmarket, Ontario, I had the blessing of meeting thousands of people over the years. I sold "Unique Gifts to Inspire and Uplift the Spirit." Part of that inspiration was to sell angel items. Interestingly, it didn't matter what religion people followed in their lives, everyone believed in three main components: #1, they all believed in a higher power #2, they all believed in some form of messengers between heaven and earth, and #3 they all believed in humans having a spiritual experience while on earth. Everything else was custom to that religion. People could be Bahia, Hindu, Christian, Hebrew, or so forth, but they all carried a similar belief system. After all these years, I no longer hold any judgment towards a religion and their beliefs. Ultimately, we all believe the same thing. We are all one. We are all connected to a Divine Source.

The Violet colour of the crown chakra gives us that frequency of belief. It provides us with the Divine food for the soul. When we surrender and release our daily challenges to the Divine, we open up this chakra to receive all the love, support, guidance and direction we need to get through our day and our life. We are not separate from the Divine, we are one of the same. When we open ourselves up to receiving that energy, miracles happen.

How many times have you seen a motivational speaker or teacher who has been through challenging times but has found the blessing that lies within the curse? People who have no arms but can still paint pictures? People with severe autism who can still write books? People who are blind or deaf but can still play music? The list goes on and on. Those are the big miracles we see and recognize, however there are many small miracles that occur every minute of the day. Friends are reunited. Babies are born. Doctors perform surgery. People fall in love. If you really want to see miracles in your life simply surrender and release your problems to the higher power.

Picture life as a school. The earth is one giant school system full of all different levels of learning. No level is better or worse than another – just different. In this school, we were given free will to make our own choices and decisions. Our school is full of ups and downs, challenges, suffering, blessings, good times and bad times. Through life we acquire beliefs, values, thoughts and feelings, which shape who we are. In this school, our greatest conflicts are our greatest teachers. Most of us are faced with a conflict and we bring up the negative responses, such as fear, expectations, judgment, guilt, excuses, blame and denial. However, when we realize that we are really connected to a higher source full of love and light and we surrender and release our conflicts to that source, we'll find the teachings and the lessons in the conflicts so our reactions are different and lead us to a more positive outcome.

For example, a client of mine was always having money troubles. She was a beautiful girl full of love and light, however she struggled with money. Each time the rent was due, she scrambled to find the money on time. After working with me one on one, we came to realize that her greatest conflict was her greatest teacher. Her parents used to say things like, "Life's always a struggle" and, "Things won't come to you easily. You have to work really hard in this world to survive." Her upbringing gave her the thoughts and beliefs that life is hard and money doesn't come easily. She was going through life finding that everything was hard work: money, relationships, finding a job she loved. Because she was brought up to believe in hardships, rather than abundance coming easily, she felt unworthy. She began to believe that she never worked hard enough or tried long enough. She was exhausted from life. How could she experience abundance when she believed that she'd never achieve it? When she realized this conditioning was from her upbringing and not what she truly believed in her soul, she was able to put forgiveness around the issue and surrender and release her conflict to the Divine Source. She began to ask for the money she needed to come to her in amazing ways. Soon, she found her life turning around. Friends asked her to do some contract work at home and she made extra money. She made connections with new people, which led her to an amazing career in hospitality, which was perfect for her personality and allowed her to spread her love and light to the world. Rent was not only paid on time, but she was even able to save her extra money and purchase her first home! If she hadn't of had the money conflict, she wouldn't have realized that she owned negative thoughts and feelings towards money and abundance, and ultimately she would have continued suffering. By becoming aware, acknowledging the issue, and releasing it to the Divine, she opened herself up to receive the love and guidance she needed in order to move forward.

Regardless of your belief system, believe in something that's bigger and contains more love than anything else you can conceive. Trust that belief and watch your life change. Transformation will occur, and love will permeate your life. The Divine universe wants you to grow, learn, and transform your spirit. We can continue to stay stuck in our 'stuff' or we can choose to bring in the universal energy by using the colour Violet to open our crown chakra and watch miracles happen.

Challenge:

Have you ever made a vision board? It is a powerful tool helping you to visualize and manifest your dreams and desires with the law of attraction.
Start journaling what goals you have and what you want to manifest arriving in your life. Think about your physical, mental, emotional and spiritual goals.
Then begin collecting pictures, words and sayings from magazines, brochures etc. that match these goals. Cut each picture out and glue it onto a piece of Bristol board.
You are creatively crafting a large poster of all your wants and needs and visually showing the universe all you desire.
Then hang this vision board in a place you will see it day and night. Focus on the universe supporting you and sending you all you need for your highest and best good.
Do not think of "how" these wishes will arrive. All you need to do it know you are worth of receiving. Let the universe surprise you and be ready to accept the abundance. Remember to say thank you when a picture manifests.

Bring VIOLET into your life to support the Crown Chakra:

- Meditation is a beautiful way to open up the crown chakra and fill it with Divine love and light. Purchase a meditation CD or join a meditation group. It will help to open up the Brow chakra as well as the Crown chakra.

- Join a networking group that matches your belief system. Maybe it's a spiritual group or a Bible study group. Find one that matches your comfort zone and attend so that you surround yourself with the people and information you need to inspire your soul.

- Find a spot in your home that's a quiet getaway. Paint the walls violet to enhance the frequency or place a violet chair or cushion in the space. Put your special items in this place to create a sacred space where you can connect to the Divine.

- When you're feeling challenged, remember to take three deep breaths with your eyes closed. Imagine beautiful violet light shining from the heavens right into your crown chakra, filling it with the violet frequency. Feel completely connected and know that you're protected and guided.

- Listen to music that can take you to a special place. It might be meditation music, harp music, or anything that connects you to your soul.

Wear our VIOLET Amethyst gemstone angel pendant

ANGELA DACEY

CONCLUSION

Congratulations! You now have an awareness of your thoughts and feelings. Awareness is half the battle in self-development. You can't heal an issue if it is hiding and you don't know that it exists. Now you're aware not only of your thoughts and feelings, but where that energy resides in your body. It's like seeing that crayon box, knowing it's a part of your surroundings when you may have never noticed it sitting on the shelf before.

With awareness being 50 percent of the healing, acknowledgement of the issues is the next 25 percent. Are you willing to now acknowledge that change needs to happen? Are you ready to get unstuck in your life and begin making shifts to embrace health on all levels? Picture yourself now holding the crayon box, absorbing the multitude of colour potential. Your whole being knows that each colour will help you with a specific thought or feeling. Each colour is food for the soul and will nourish you in your healing. Each colour will bring you closer to painting that masterpiece representing your life.

The last 25 percent of this picture is to take action! Pick a colour out of the box. Which colour will it be? Which thought or feeling needs to be healed and cleared so that you receive a beautiful flow of energy? Take action to heal. Attend a personal development seminar, like a workshop. Join a spiritual retreat. Read the top self-help books.

If you're unsure where to start, actually use the crayon box. Pull out the first colour that attracts your attention. Is it red or orange, representing the physical chakras? Maybe yellow beckoning you to focus on your mental health. Is your emotional energy center calling for attention with a shade of green or blue? Have the purples said, "Pick me" so that you work on your spiritual chakras? The colour you choose will innately show you where you need to begin your work.

You may be asking, "What if I picked black, white or pink?"

White is all the colours combined. If you hold a crystal prism up into the sunlight you will see a beautiful rainbow. Each colour from that rainbow has a frequency or energy. Reds vibrate slowly and with warmth. Violets vibrate fast and cool. Just as nature's rainbows encompass all the colours, so do we with our chakras. Rainbows say take care of the physical, mental, emotional and spiritual self. Therefore, if you are attracted to white, consider it to be Divine. It is the highest power saying, "Heal yourself one colour at a time." We've used the WHITE Mother of Pearl in our gemstone angel pendant for divine wisdom and guidance.

Black, on the other hand, is a resistance to colour. Black pushes energy away. If you chose black as your main colour, you may want to hide your true self and are resistant to healing. Black suppresses the emotions so energy will not flow. Have you ever seen someone all dressed in black? Do they seem easy to approach and willing to open up authentically to you? Chances are you will not get to see the inner beauty of that person shine. If you are someone who wears black every day, try adding one element of colour to your style. A colourful piece of jewellery, a coloured tie, or maybe different coloured shoes is a great place to start. Add a little bit of colour and notice if you feel more alive and open. If you are uncomfortable, feeling as though you are drawing more attention to yourself, use that as awareness and acknowledge the thought or feeling. Then take action to begin to shift that perspective.

Pink is a beautiful colour as it as the universe is giving all the chakras a hug. Pink relates to the bottom red root chakra and also to the top violet crown chakra. Pink is like the vitamins and minerals needed for ultimate self love / self worth. It is the colour of kindness, softness, it calms anger and aggression and connects us to our feminine energy. We've used the PINK Rose Quartz in our gemstone angel pendant.

Colour is an amazing tool awaiting to be used in our healing. Luckily, colour is everywhere. Understanding the basics of colour therapy, you now have the power to shift your thoughts and feelings towards passion, joy, courage, balance, truth, inner peace, and belief.

We are given colour in nature, art, clothing, jewelry…everywhere! Use it to your advantage. You now have a powerful gift.

Enjoy the journey and

Live Life Colourfully!

THANK YOU

Launching this first book has been a blessing. Years ago, while teaching my courses, I was asked many times, "Where's the book?" I began writing it in little coffee shops all over Newmarket, Ontario. Then, my life as I knew it, fell apart. With my son becoming ill with Epilepsy, a divorce from my highschool sweetheart and the sudden passing of my Dad, the manuscript sat in my computer, untouched.

Now through the grief and healing, I am once again Living Life Colourfully! With my spiritual faith being the forefront in my life, I was guided to reopen the manuscript, edit the work and launch the beginning of a new direction in my life. Having the tools and techniques combined with the colour psychology knowledge made the transitions and healing an easier, more insightful process. I pray that the suggestions in this book, combined with the colour energy knowledge, will help you detox your thoughts and feelings and live your life more colourfully!

I'd like to thank a few people who have proven to be earth angels in my life and inspired me to keep moving forward.

Evan and Linnea, waking up each day knowing that I'm the mom of two phenomenal children makes life exceptional. Seeing your smiling faces, knowing the love we share and watching you both grow into beautiful human beings is my greatest gift. You make me want to continuously live my life purpose and serve for the highest good.

Natalie and Rodney Muir, how can I thank you? Words are not enough. You are forever my soul family.

Bernard Fealing, your compassion, kindness, love and support uplifts my spirits every day. You always help me find my colourful light in my darkest days. Thank you for constantly seeing me as a superhero!

Ron Clifford, your calm nature, wise advice, open heart and encouragement makes every day we work together a brighter day. I love sharing our progression in business and life together. You are truly a mentor!

To every friend and family member that has offered love and support, I thank you.

I also want to thank every coffee shop that has allowed me to sit in their environment for hours without complaint. Americanos, comfy couches and background music makes the best office!

Enjoy the journey and have fun learning even more how to

Live Life Colourfully!

Colourfully Yours,

Angela

ANGELA DACEY
(AUTHOR)

Angela Dacey's mission is to help you "Detox Your Thoughts™ and Live Life Colourfully™ both personally and professionally.

After 20+ years, Angela's background in colour psychology, personal development and business has led her to be a sought after professional speaker, trainer, consultant and life advisor. She has been interviewed around the world in all forms of media for her knowledge and insight.

Angela is a blessed, mother of two children, Evan & Linnea and Cashew the family dog ☺ She resides in Newmarket, Ontario, Canada.

She can be reached personally at angela@livelifecolourfully.com

www.livelifecolourfully.com

LES LUXEMBURGER
(BOOK COVER ART)

 Les is a dynamic, energetic visual artist who has been actively creating artwork since the age of six. He vividly recounts waking up one morning and having the desire to create comic books! Starting with cartoon characters, Les created several comic books, and wrote his first Fantasy novel at the age of 13. When Les entered high school, his artistic practice evolved to include painting, drawing and pastel, focusing on such subject matter as portraits, still life, wildlife, and abstract concepts.

Les immersed himself in art programs throughout his high school years, and well as into university and his adult life. It was at Sheridan College, ON that Les' skills as a visual artist really shined and bloomed and his style became more open, fluid, experimental and playful. Leslie went on to study at several prominent art schools in Ontario including: Mississauga Valley School of Art, Maxx the Mutt Animation school, and eventually Newmarket School of Art, where he taught fine art in 2011.

Since then, Les completed a Bachelor (with Honours) and Master Degree in Environmental Studies from York University, and has merged both of his passions and specializations: visual art, and the natural environment, sustainability and conservation.

luxeartstudio@gmail.com

KATHY HOUSE
(RED PICTURE)

Photographic Artist

Kathy House has worked in the advertising business for over 25 years on several prestigious, multi-national accounts.

Kathy has recently focused her photographic skills and has developed a unique, signature style of photographic art.

Her published works include an award-winning Muskoka historical book and multimedia advertising communications. Kathy's vibrant photographic art has been acquired by enthusiastic collectors across North America, South Africa and Europe.

www.facebook.com/KathyHousePhotoArt

NAVID BAKTASH
(ORANGE & YELLOW PICTURE)

 Navid's passion for photography grew with the start of developing photos through a pinhole box camera. Soon after completing a degree in life sciences, he went on a journey with his camera around different parts of the world. Learning about different cultures and focusing on nature, he began to appreciate the concept of relationships between people and nature. Through images, he hopes to create a portal for human relationships as a way of bringing us closer together, conveying the idea that we all are interconnected and that is the very soul of human existence. His work focuses on people, cultures, landscape and wildlifephotography.

www.illuminatophotography.com

VICKIE SPARKS
(GREEN & INDIGO PICTURE)

 In all things for nature there is something of the marvelous - and that is what Vickie Sparks strives to capture in her photography. Vickie is an amateur photographer who has a passion for all things creative! A native of England, Vickie has lived in Canada for more than half her life and is inspired by the simplicity and complexity of the world around us.

sunsetrock@hotmail.com

RON CLIFFORD
(VIOLET PIC & ANGELA'S BIO PICS)

Anyone who knows Ron Clifford knows that while he is a skilled, award-winning photographer, he is first and foremost an encourager, a mentor and an educator. Call him an "Inspirologist" He has made a career out of encouraging the creative soul in others. As a result of his commitment to building strong communities, he has his work featured on Google products and has been featured in National Geographic's online community. Ron has become well known for his involvement in online and in-person mentoring in photography, life and business and has been inspiring fellow creatives and entrepreneurs through talks, presentations and workshops. Recently he was able to share his story about overcoming on the TEDx stage. Along with teaching online, Ron is also a Photography Guide leading unique photography symposiums workshops and tours to some of the most remote places on earth. In Ron's own words, "I always say, do what you can't help but do. And for me, that is to explore the natural world, photograph the people and places in it, and teach others to do the same."

www.ronclifford.com

Colourfully Yours,

Angela

Made in the USA
Lexington, KY
30 October 2019